WHY

WE

Other booklets from *Questions of Life* include:

Christianity: Boring, Untrue or Irrelevant?
Who Is Jesus?
Why Did Jesus Die?
How Can I Be Sure of My Faith?
Why and How Should I Read the Bible?
Why and How Do I Pray?
How Does God Guide Us?
The Holy Spirit
How Can I Resist Evil
Why and How Should We Tell Others?
Does God Heal Today?
How Can I Make the Most of the Rest of My Life?

Other booklets from *Searching Issues* include:

Why Does God Allow Suffering?
What About Other Religions?
Is There Anything Wrong with Sex Before Marriage?
How Does the New Age Movement Relate to Christianity?
Is the Trinity Unbiblical, Unbelievable and Irrelevant?
Is there a Conflict Between Science and Christianity?
What Is the Christian Attitude to Homosexuality?

Why and How
Should we
Tell Others?

NICKY GUMBEL

Alpha

Text cartoons by Charlie Mackesy
Cover artwork by Glenn Andrews

ISBN 1 84291 203 8

2 3 4 5 6 7   09 08 07 06

Published by
KINGSWAY COMMUNICATIONS LTD
Lottbridge Drove, Eastbourne BN23 6NT, England.
Email: books@kingsway.co.uk
Printed in Canada

Contents

Why and How Should We
Tell Others?

Why should we talk about our Christian faith? Isn't it a private matter? Isn't the best sort of Christian the one who just lives the Christian life? Sometimes people say to me, 'I know someone [usually their mother or their aunt] who is a Christian. They have a really strong faith – but they do not talk about it. Isn't that the highest form of Christianity?'

The short answer is that someone must have told them about the Christian faith. The slightly longer answer is that there are good reasons for telling others about Jesus. First, it is a command of Jesus himself. Tom Forrest, the Roman Catholic priest who first suggested to the Pope the idea of calling the 1990s 'The Decade of Evangelism', points out that the word 'go' appears 1,514 times in the Bible (RSV), 233 times in the New Testament and 54 times in Matthew's Gospel. Jesus tells us to 'go':

'Go to the lost sheep …'
'Go and tell John …'

'Go and invite all you meet ...'

'Go and make disciples ...'

Indeed, these are the last recorded words of Jesus in Matthew's Gospel:

> Then Jesus came to them and said, 'All authority in heaven and on earth has been given to me. Therefore go and make disciples of all nations, baptising them in the name of the Father and of the Son and of the Holy Spirit, and teaching them to obey everything I have commanded you. And surely I will be with you always, to the very end of the age' (Matthew 28:18–20).

Secondly, we tell people because there is a desperate need for people to hear the good news of Jesus Christ. If we were in the Sahara Desert and had discovered an oasis, it would be extremely selfish not to tell the people around us who were thirsty where their thirst could be satisfied. Jesus is the only One who can satisfy the thirsty hearts of men and women. Often the recognition of this thirst comes from surprising sources. The singer, Sinead O'Connor, said in an interview: 'As a race we feel empty. This is because our spirituality has been wiped out and we don't know how to express ourselves. As a result we're encouraged to fill that gap with alcohol, drugs, sex or money. People out there are screaming for the truth.'

Thirdly, we tell others because, having discovered the good news ourselves, we feel an urgent desire to pass it on. If we have received good news we want to tell others. When our first child was born, my wife Pippa gave me a list of about ten people to ring. The first person I rang was her mother. I told her that we had a son and that he and Pippa were well. I then tried ringing my mother, but the phone was engaged. The third person on the list was Pippa's sister. By the time I had telephoned her she had already heard the news from Pippa's mother and so had all the others on the list. My mother's phone had been engaged because Pippa's mother was ringing her with the news. Good news travels fast. I did not need to implore Pippa's mother to pass on the message. She was bursting to tell them all. When we appreciate what good news the gospel is, we shall be bursting to tell others.

But how do we go about telling others? It seems to me that there are two opposite dangers. First, there is the danger of insensitivity. When I first became a Christian I fell into this. I was so excited about what had happened that I longed for everyone else to follow suit. After I had been a Christian for a few days I went to a party, determined to tell everyone. I saw a friend dancing and decided the first step was to make her realise her need. So I went up to her and said, 'You look awful. You really need Jesus.' She thought that I had gone mad. It was not the most effective way of telling someone the good news! (However, she did later become a Christian – quite independently of me, and she is now my wife!)

The next party I went to I decided to go well equipped. So I got hold of a number of booklets, Christian books on various issues and a New Testament. I stuffed them into every pocket I could find. Somehow I managed to find a girl who was willing to dance with me. It was hard going with so many books in my pocket, so I asked if we could sit down. I soon brought the subject round to Christianity. For every question she asked, I was able to produce a book from my pocket on exactly that subject. Eventually she went away with an armful of books. The next day she was going to France and was reading one of the books I had given her on the boat. Suddenly she understood the truth of what Jesus had done for her and, turning to her neighbour, she said, 'I have just become a Christian.' She died in a riding accident at the age of twenty-one. It was wonderful that she had come to Christ before she died – even though I don't think I went about it in quite the right way.

If we charge around like a bull in a china shop, sooner or later we get hurt. Even if we approach the subject sensitively, we may still get hurt. When we do, we tend to withdraw. Certainly this was my experience. After a few years, I moved from the danger of insensitivity and fell into the opposite danger of fear. There was a time (ironically it was when I was at theological college) when I became fearful of even talking about Jesus to those who were not Christians. On one occasion, a group of us went from the college to a parish mission on the outskirts of Liverpool, to tell people the good news. Each night we had supper with different people from the parish. One night a friend of mine called Rupert and I were sent to supper with a couple who were on the fringe of the church (or, to be more accurate, the wife was on the fringe and the husband was not a churchgoer). Halfway through the main course the husband asked me what we were doing up there. I stumbled, stammered, hesitated and prevaricated. He kept on repeating the question. Eventually Rupert said straight out, 'We have come here to tell people about Jesus.' I felt deeply embarrassed and hoped the ground would swallow us all up! I realised how frozen with fear I had become and that I was afraid even to take the name of Jesus on my lips.

In order to avoid these dangers of insensitivity and fear, we need to realise that telling others about Jesus arises out of our own relationship with God. It is a natural part of that relationship. As we walk with God, it should be quite natural for us to talk to people about that relationship in co-operation with the Spirit of God.

I find it helpful to think of this subject under five headings – all beginning with the letter 'p' – presence, persuasion, proclamation, power and prayer.

PRESENCE

Jesus said to his disciples:

> You are the salt of the earth. But if the salt loses its saltiness, how can it be made salty again? It is no longer good for anything, except to be thrown out and trampled under foot. You are the light of the world. A city on a hill cannot be hidden. Neither do people light a lamp and put it under a bowl. Instead they put it on its stand, and it gives light to everyone in the house. In the same way, let your light shine before others, that they may see your good deeds and praise your Father in heaven (Matthew 5:13–16).

Jesus calls us to have a wide-ranging influence ('salt of the *earth*' and 'the light of the *world*'). In order to exercise this influence, we need to be 'in the world' (at work, in our neighbourhood and among our family and friends) and not to withdraw into what John Stott calls our 'elegant little ecclesiastical salt cellars'.

11

Yet we are called to be different – to live a radically different lifestyle from the world, so that we may be effective as salt and light in it.

We are called first to be salt. In centuries before refrigeration was invented salt was used to keep meat wholesome and to prevent decay. We are called as Christians to stop society going bad. We do this by our words, as we speak out about moral standards and moral issues, and as we use our influence to bring about God's standards in society around us. We do it by our deeds as we play our part as citizens, aiming to create better social structures, working for justice, freedom and dignity for the individual, and by helping to abolish discrimination. We do it also by our social action to help those who are casualties of our society. To this end, some Christians are called to get involved in local or national politics. Others are called to spend their lives like Mother Teresa and Jackie Pullinger 'ministering *with* the poor' (to use Jackie Pullinger's expression). All of us are called to play a part in this to a greater or lesser extent.

Secondly, Jesus calls us to be light – to allow the light of Christ to shine through us. We do this by what Jesus calls 'your good deeds' – everything that we do or say because we are Christians. They can be summarised as 'loving our neighbour as ourselves'.

Living out the Christian life is the most appropriate way of passing on the good news to those who live in very close proximity to us. This certainly applies to our family, colleagues at work and flatmates. If they know we are Christians, that fact alone puts them under a degree of pressure. To be continually speaking about our faith may backfire. They are more likely to be affected by genuine love and concern. At work people should notice our consistency, honesty, truthfulness, hard work, reliability, avoidance of gossip and desire to encourage other people. At home, parents, family and flatmates will be influenced by our service to others, our patience and our kindness, far more than by our words.

This is of great importance if one's husband or wife is not a Christian. Peter encouraged Christian wives that if any of them have husbands who 'do not believe the word, they may be won over without talk by the behaviour of their wives, when they see the purity and reverence of your lives' (1 Peter 3:1, italics mine).

Bruce and Geraldine Streather were married in December 1973. When Geraldine came to Christ in 1981, Bruce was not remotely interested. Bruce was a busy lawyer and a very keen golfer: he used to play most weekends. He never came to church.

For ten years Geraldine prayed for him and lived out the Christian life in front of him. She did not put any pressure on him and did not engage in any arguments about it. Over the years, Bruce was struck by her extraordinary kindness and consideration, especially to his mother whose cancer and related illnesses made her increasingly difficult. Eventually, in 1991, she invited him to come to an Alpha supper. Bruce came, and decided to come on the following Alpha course.

Geraldine wrote to me afterwards saying, 'I cried all the way home and prayed, telling God that as I had got Bruce to Alpha, he must do the rest. When Bruce returned from the first night of the course, I only asked him if he had enjoyed himself.'

On week seven of the course, Bruce gave his life to Christ and by the end he was the most enthusiastic Christian one could ever meet. I asked Geraldine what it was like living with him now. She replied, 'It's a bit like living with Billy Graham!'

Her letter continued: 'He tells everyone about Jesus. Instead of trying not to mention Christianity in front of friends when Bruce was there, in case it harmed our marriage, at every dinner party he talks to people about God and I am left at the other end listening to what he is saying. It seems that all my prayers have been answered. Last March I told God that I was fed up with Bruce not being a Christian. I told him I didn't care what happened to our house or money as long as Bruce became a Christian. Life will never be the same again – thank God for that.'

Nevertheless, being 'lights in the world' does not just involve our lifestyle. It also involves our lips. Our family, our flatmates and our colleagues will eventually ask questions about our faith. It is often better to wait until they do. If we are asked, we should always be prepared to give an answer. Peter writes: 'Always be prepared to give an answer to everyone who asks you to give the reason for the hope that you have. But do this with gentleness and respect' (1 Peter 3:15).

When we do get opportunities to speak, how do we go about it?

Persuasion

Many people today have objections to the Christian faith or, at least, questions which they want answered before they are ready to come to faith in Christ. They need to be persuaded about the truth. Paul was willing to try to persuade people. He regarded it as his duty out of love for them: 'Since, then, we know what it is to fear the Lord, we try to *persuade* people' (2 Corinthians 5:11, italics mine).

When he went to Thessalonica he 'reasoned', 'explained' and 'proved' from the Scriptures that the Christ had to suffer and rise from the dead: '… some of the Jews were persuaded …' (Acts 17:4). In Corinth, while working on tents during the week, 'every Sabbath he reasoned in the synagogue, trying to persuade Jews and Greeks' (Acts 18:4).

During the course of conversations about the Christian faith, objections will often be raised and we need to be equipped to deal with these. On one occasion, Jesus was talking to a woman about the mess her life was in (John 4). Then he offered her eternal life. At that moment she raised a theological question about places of worship. He answered it, but quickly brought the conversation back to the essential issue. This is a good example for us to follow.

Usually when people raise theological questions and objections, they are genuinely looking for the answers. The most common questions which I get asked are, 'Why does God allow suffering?' and, 'What about other religions?' But there are a whole range of other questions. These may be serious, and may require a serious answer. Sometimes, however, these questions can be a smokescreen to avoid the real issue. Such people are put off becoming Christians, not by the theological objections, but by the moral ones. They are not willing to give their lives to Christ for fear of the change of lifestyle that Christianity will involve.

On the mission which I mentioned earlier, Rupert and I went to speak at a meeting about our Christian faith. After we had spoken, a university lecturer raised a large number of questions and objections. I didn't know where to begin to answer them all. Rupert simply asked, 'If we could answer all your questions satisfactorily, would you become a Christian?' He replied, very honestly, 'No.' So there didn't seem a great deal of point in answering what for him were purely academic enquiries. But when the questions are genuine, reasoning, explaining and proving form an important part of telling others about Jesus.

PROCLAMATION

The heart of telling others is the proclamation of the good news of Jesus Christ. It is announcing, communicating and proclaiming the Christian faith to those outside the faith. There are many ways in which this can be done. One of the most effective ways is bringing people to hear the gospel explained by someone else. This can often be more advisable, especially in the early stages of our Christian lives, than trying to explain the gospel ourselves.

Many who come to faith in Christ have lots of friends who have little or no connection with the church. This provides an excellent opportunity to say to these friends, as Jesus did on one occasion, 'Come … and you will see' (John 1:39). A woman in her twenties recently became a Christian and started coming to church in London. At weekends, however, she would stay with her parents in Wiltshire, and she then insisted on leaving them at 3 pm on Sunday afternoon in order to be in time for church. One Sunday evening she got stuck in a bad traffic jam on the Hammersmith flyover and could not get to the evening service. She was so upset that she burst into tears. She went round to see some friends, who did not even know she had become a Christian. They asked her what was wrong. She answered through the tears, 'I've missed church.' They were totally mystified. The next Sunday they all came to see what they were missing! One of them came to Christ very shortly afterwards.

There is no greater privilege and no greater joy than enabling someone to find out about Jesus Christ. The former Archbishop of Canterbury, William Temple, wrote his commentary on John's Gospel while on his knees, asking God to speak to his heart. When he came to the words, 'And he [Andrew] brought Simon to Jesus' (John 1:42), he wrote a short but momentous sentence: 'The greatest service that one man can render another.'

We don't hear much more about Andrew except that he was always bringing people to Jesus (John 6:8; 12:22). But Simon Peter his brother went on to be one of the greatest influences in the history of Christianity. We cannot all be Simon Peters, but we can all do what Andrew did – we can bring someone to Jesus.

Albert McMakin was a twenty-four-year-old farmer who had recently come to faith in Christ. He was so full of enthusiasm that he filled a truck with people and took them to a meeting to hear about Jesus. There was a good-looking farmer's son whom he was especially keen to get to a meeting, but this young man was hard to persuade – he was busy falling in and out of love with different girls, and did not seem to be attracted to Christianity. Eventually, Albert McMakin managed to persuade him to come by asking him to drive the truck. When they arrived, Albert's guest decided to go in and was 'spellbound' and began to have thoughts he had never known before. He went back again and again until one night, he went forward and gave his life to Jesus Christ. That man, the driver of the truck, was Billy Graham. The year was 1934. Since then Billy Graham has led thousands to faith in Jesus Christ. We cannot all be like Billy Graham, but we can all be like Albert McMakin – we can all bring our friends to Jesus.

Sometimes we are given the opportunity to explain the gospel ourselves. One good way of doing this is to tell the story of what has happened to us. We see a biblical model in Paul's testimony in Acts 26:9–23. It falls into three parts: he speaks about what he was like before (vv. 9–11), what it meant to meet Jesus (vv. 12–15) and what it has meant for him since (vv. 19–23). When explaining what someone has to do to become a Christian, a framework can be helpful. There are many different ways of presenting the gospel. I have set out the method I use in a booklet called *Why Jesus?*.

One man in our church told me recently about how he had come to Christ. He was going through difficulties in his business and had to go to the United States on a business trip. He was not feeling very happy as he rode in a taxi to the airport. On the dashboard of the taxi he noticed pictures of the taxi driver's children. He could not see the face of the driver, but he asked him about his family. He felt great love coming from the man. As the conversation went on, the taxi driver said to him, 'I sense that you are not happy. If you believe in Christ it makes all the difference.'

The businessman said to me, 'Here was a man speaking with authority. I thought I was the one in authority. After all, I was paying.' The taxi driver said to him eventually, 'Don't you think it's time you settled all this by accepting Christ?' They arrived at the airport. For the first time the taxi driver turned round and the businessman saw his face – it was full of kindness. He said to him, 'Why don't we pray? If you want Christ in your life, ask him.' They prayed together and the driver gave him a booklet about the Christian faith. The taxi driver was a modest unassuming person who was there one moment and gone the next, but he had taken the opportunity to proclaim the good news of Jesus Christ. This changed the whole course of a man's life.

POWER

In the New Testament the proclamation of the gospel is often accompanied by a demonstration of the power of God. Jesus came proclaiming: 'The kingdom of God is near. Repent and believe the good news!' (Mark 1:15). Jesus went on to demonstrate the power of the gospel by the expulsion of evil (Mark 1:21–28) and by healing the sick (Mark 1:29–34, 40–45).

Jesus told his disciples to do what he had been doing. He told them to do the works of the kingdom – 'to heal the sick who are there' and to proclaim the good news – and to tell them, 'The kingdom of God is near you' (Luke 10:9). As we read on in the Gospels and Acts we see that that is what they did. Paul wrote to the Thessalonians: 'Our gospel came to you not simply with words, but also with power' (1 Thessalonians 1:5).

Proclamation and demonstration go hand in hand. Often one leads to the other. On one occasion Peter and John were on their way to church. Outside was a man crippled from birth. He had been sitting there for years. He asked for money. Peter said, in effect, 'I am sorry. I haven't got any money, but I will give you what I have. In the name of Jesus Christ of Nazareth, walk.' He took his hand and helped him up. Instantly, he jumped to his feet and began to walk. When he realised he was healed, he leapt and jumped and praised God (Acts 3:1–10).

Everyone knew that this man had been crippled for years, and a huge crowd gathered around. After the demonstration of the power of God came the proclamation of the gospel. People were asking, 'How did this happen?' Peter was able to tell them all about Jesus: 'It is Jesus' name and the faith that comes through him that has given this complete healing to him, as you can all see' (Acts 3:16). I examine this area in more detail by looking at the nature of the kingdom of God and the place of healing in it in my booklet 'Does God Heal Today?'.

PRAYER

We have already seen the importance that prayer had in the life of Jesus. While he was proclaiming and demonstrating the gospel he was also praying (Mark 1:35–37). Prayer is essential in the area of telling others the good news.

We need to pray for blind eyes to be opened. Many people are blinded to the gospel (2 Corinthians 4:4). They can see physically, but they cannot see the spiritual world. We need to pray that the Spirit of God will open the eyes of the blind so that they can understand the truth about Jesus.

Most of us find, when we come to faith in Christ, that there has been somebody praying for us. It may be a member of the family, a godparent or a friend. There will be somebody, I suspect, in nearly every case who has been praying that our eyes will be opened to see the truth. James Hudson Taylor, who founded the China Inland Mission, influenced millions for Jesus Christ. He was brought up in Yorkshire and became a rebellious teenager. One day, when his mother was away and his sister was out, he picked up a Christian book, intending to read the story and skip the moral. He curled up in the barn behind the house and began to read.

As he read, he was struck by the phrase 'the finished work of Christ'. He thought Christianity to be a dreary struggle to pay off bad debts with good. He had long since abandoned the struggle. He owed too much. He sought simply to have a good time. This phrase broke open his mind to a sudden certainty that Christ, by his death on the cross, had already discharged this debt of sins: 'And with this dawned the joyful conviction, as light was flashed into my soul by the Holy Spirit, that there was nothing in the world to be done but to fall down on one's knees and accepting this Saviour and His Salvation, to praise Him for evermore.' No Luther, Bunyan or Wesley had a more complete sense of the rolling away of his burden, of light dismissing darkness, of rebirth and the close friendship of Christ, than did Hudson Taylor on that June afternoon in 1849 at the age of seventeen.

Ten days later his mother came home. He ran to the door 'to tell her I had such glad news to give'. She replied as she hugged him, 'I know, my boy. I have been rejoicing for a fortnight in the glad tidings you have to tell me.' Hudson was amazed. She had been eighty miles away, and on the very day of the incident in the barn she had felt such an overwhelming desire to pray for Hudson that she had spent hours on her knees, and had arisen with the unshakeable conviction that her prayers had been answered. He never forgot the importance of prayer.[1]

When a friend of mine, Ric, became a Christian he rang a friend whom he knew to be a Christian as well, and told him what had happened. The friend replied, 'I have been praying for you for four years.' Ric then started to pray for one of his own friends, and within ten weeks he too became a Christian.

We need to pray for our friends. We also need to pray for ourselves. When we talk to people about Jesus, we may sometimes get a negative reaction. The temptation at that moment is to give up. When Peter and John healed the crippled man and proclaimed the gospel, they were arrested and threatened with dire consequences should they continue. At times, they got a decidedly negative reaction; but they did not give up. Rather, they prayed – not for protection, but for boldness in preaching the gospel and for God to perform more signs and wonders through the name of Jesus (Acts 4:29–31).

It is vital for all of us as Christians to persevere in telling others about Jesus – by our presence, persuasion, proclamation, power and prayer. If we do, over the course of a lifetime we shall see many lives changed.

During the war a man was shot and lay dying in the trenches. A friend leaned over to him and said, 'Is there anything I can do for you?'

He replied, 'No, I am dying.'

'Is there anyone I can send a message to for you?'

'Yes, you can send a message to this man at this address. Tell him that in my last minutes what he taught me as a child is helping me to die.'

The man was his old Sunday school teacher. When the message got back to him, he said, 'God forgive me. I gave up Sunday school teaching years ago because I thought I was getting nowhere. I thought it was no use.'

When we tell people about Jesus, it is never 'no use'. For the gospel 'is the power of God for the salvation of everyone who believes' (Romans 1:16).

Note

1. J. C. Pollock, *Hudson Taylor and Maria* (Hodder & Stoughton, 1978).

.

Study Guide

1. What answer would you give to someone who says that Christianity is 'a private matter' (p. 7)?
2. What are the 'two opposite dangers' that Nicky describes (p. 9)?
3. What does it mean in practice to be 'salt' and 'light' to those around us (p. 11)?
4. How can we be better equipped to answer the opbligations that people may have to the Christian faith (p. 15)?
5. What are the ways in which we might 'bring people to jesus' (p. 16)?
6. 'Prayer is essential in the area of telling others the good news' (pp. 20f). Why?
7. How should we respond when we get 'negative reactions' to speaking about jesus (p. 22)?

Alpha

This book is an Alpha resource. The Alpha course is a practical introduction to the Christian faith initiated by Holy Trinity Brompton in London, and now being run by thousands of churches throughout the UK as well as overseas.

For more information on Alpha, and details of tapes, videos and training manuals, contact the Alpha office, Holy Trinity Brompton on 0207 581 8255, (home page: http://www.alpha.org), or STL, PO Box 300, Kingstown Broadway, Carlisle, Cumbria CA3 0QS.

Alpha Hotline for telephone orders:
0845 7581 278 (all calls at local rate)

To order from overseas:
Tel +44 1228 611749
Fax +44 1228 514949

Email: alpha@stl.org

Alpha

Alpha titles available

Alpha: Questions of Life   The Alpha course in book form. In fifteen compelling chapters Nicky Gumbel points the way to an authentic Christianity which is exciting and relevant to todays world. Also available as booklets.

Searching Issues   The seven issues most often raised by participants on the Alpha course: suffering, other religions, sex before marriage, the New Age, homosexuality, science and Christianity, and the Trinity. Also available as booklets.

A Life Worth Living   What happens after Alpha? Based on the book of Philippians, this is an invaluable next step for those who have just completed the Alpha course, and for anyone eager to put their faith on a firm biblical footing.

How to Run the Alpha Course: Telling Others   The theological principles and the practical details of how courses are run. Each alternate chapter consists of a testimony of someone whose life has been changed by God through an Alpha course.

Challenging Lifestyle   Studies in the Sermon on the Mount showing how Jesus' teaching flies in the face of modern lifestyle and presents us with a radical alternative.

The Heart of Revival   Ten Bible studies based on the book of Isaiah, drawing out important truths for today by interpreting some of the teaching of the Old Testament prophet Isaiah. The book seeks to understand what revival might mean and how we can prepare to be part of it.

30 Days   Nicky Gumbel selects thirty passages from the Old and New Testament which can be read over thirty days. It is designed for those on an Alpha course and others who are interested in beginning to explore the Bible.

Why Jesus?   A booklet – given to all participants at the start of the Alpha course. 'The clearest, best illustrated and most challenging short presentation of Jesus that I know.' – Michael Green

All titles are by Nicky Gumbel, who is vicar of
Holy Trinity Brompton